MOON POETRY

Cartography of Shadows and Silver Lights
A Lyrical Moon Night Journey

EDUARD SCHMIDT-ZORNER

MOON POETRY

Cartography of Shadows and Silver Lights
A Lyrical Moon Night Journey

Eduard Schmidt-Zorner

IMPRESSUM

ISBN: 978-93-6354-633-2

Published by Rochak Publishing
Printed by Repro India.

Cover Photo Author
Photo last page Author
Author Photos Barbara Derbyshire (2) Own author's Photo (1)

Disclaimer

This is a work of creative expression. All poems in this collection are works of fiction, inspired by imagination, emotion, and artistic interpretation. Any resemblance to actual persons, living or dead, or real events is purely coincidental. The views and opinions expressed in the poems are those of the author and do not reflect those of any individual or organization.

Poems are often written on moonlit nights

CONTENTS

INTRODUCTION

Moon poetry is not loud, not harsh like hot sunshine or boiling heat. Moon poetry is subtle, soft, like a silvery shine.

On the 13th of January 2025, the date I started this book, we could see the full Wolf Moon accompanied by Mars.

The moon has forever been a mirror to the human soul—quiet, watchful, and distant, the soft guardian of the night, a silver thread stitching together sky and silence. In its glow, time slows, and the world slips into a gentler rhythm.

This collection of moon poetry is a passage through stillness, observation, and gentle nights. Here, the moon is more than a celestial body—it is an ancient muse, a keeper of secrets, and a silent witness to longing, wonder, and an unspoken language.

I wrote these poems in the hush of midnight, reflecting the mysticism of lunar cycles, and the eternal dance between light and dark.

Each verse seeks not to explain the moon but to feel it—to breathe in its pale magic and offer it back in lines and rhythms shaped by reverence. In this gentle lunarscape, readers are invited to wander, to dream, and to remember the parts of themselves that awaken under silver skies.

Let the moon guide you now, as it always has, as a symbol, a companion. She is the light that does not blind, the silence that speaks, the rhythm by which tides and hearts both move.

Through verses threaded with silver and shadow, these poems seek to touch what cannot be grasped—how moonlight spills like thought, how it renders even sorrow beautiful. They speak in hushed voices of the mystic and the mundane: the curve of a crescent like a whispered promise, the full moon as an ancient eye gazing back with infinite understanding.

To read these poems is not just to look at the moon, but to feel her—to remember the primal awe she inspires, the quiet magic she carries, and the way she makes us all poets when we stand beneath her glow.

She does not speak, yet tells the tides
of secrets drawn in silver lines,
a lantern hung in ink-dark skies,
the dream between the days and nights.

Before I start the presentation of my moon poems, I would like to share a most perfect translation which I found, while rooting through my poetry book library, and which I, as translator and poet, highly appreciate, knowing how challenging poetry translations are:

Matthias Claudius – Abendlied (Der Mond ist aufgegangen)
Evening Song (The Moon has risen)
English translation by Bertram Kottmann

Behold, the moon has risen,
the golden stars, they glisten
upon the heavens bright.
The forests rest in shadows,
and from the quiet meadows
white hazes rise into the night.

The world in stillness clouded
and soft in twilight shrouded,
so peaceful and so fair.
Just like a chamber waiting,
where you can rest abating

the daytime's mis'ry and despair.

Behold the moon – and wonder
why half of her stands yonder,
yet she is round and fair.
We are the ones who're fooling
'cause we are ridiculing
as our minds are unaware.

We vain and wretched sinners
presume to be the winners,
but we know nothing yet.
So many neat solutions

are nought but great delusions

that farther off the path us get.

God, grant us Thy salvation!
No worldly aspiration,
no vanity allow!
Like children simple-hearted,
and joyful like we started,
let us become and teach us how!

And lastly, grant us leaving
the world without much grieving,
let peaceful be our death.
When from the earth You take us,
let heaven's joy await us
stand by us, Lord, at our last breath.

So, brothers, in His keeping
prepare yourself for sleeping;
cold is the evening breeze.
Spare us, Oh Lord, Your ire,
let rest us by the fire,
and grant our ailing neighbour peace.

My own Moon Poetry starts on the next page

WOLF MOON

Wet and grey,
mosses and lichens hang from the trees
like catafalque blankets,
still submerged in deadly winter sleep.
Remnants of snow in corners
survive for a short time.
Plants wait for spring,
for the first warm rays.

The colours are still uniform,
shades of permanent grey compete.
The light-grey sky, the dingy grey ground,
the grey-brown of the tree bark,
the dark grey of the mud.
Evening falls.

Today Mars meets the Wolf Moon…
As the sun is rising in the East,
the moon rises in the East
and sets in the West, like the Sun.
The Sun rises in the East
to open and enliven the day

and sets in the West to close the day
to dismiss us from labour
and sorrowful thoughts,
opens the curtain for the night
to give us sleep.

Just like the sun
the moon rises in the East
to guard our sleep
until it sets in the West –
a continuous change in the universe.

The mountain chain is a white band
on a grey sky cloth - like a gem,
a bright, white moon, ruler of this night,
casts silver over the green-white fields
and at his left hand
the red brilliant star Mars
skims the first full moon of the year.

In the thicket, a startled deer.
Up the field, the bark of a fox.
Elsewhere, the wolves howl
in the depth of the winter,

they continue to roam and hunt.
No wolf is howling here.
I inhale the sharp unspoiled air.
Dipped in a lake of argentum
are glens and dales.

The full moon rises higher in the sky,
Moon and Mars will get closer
throughout this night
climbing higher together
and heading towards the southeast
as midnight approaches.

A good month to observe Mars
because the winter skies are clear and dark.
Both will be heading towards the western horizon,
Mars will get ever closer to the Moon,
skimming the northern edge of the lunar disc
in the very early hours of the next day.

They rise above the eastern horizon
in the early evening,
Mars is now above and to the right of the Moon,
the two bodies getting farther apart

as the evening draws on.

The celestial tango is over.
We retire and praise him
as Stay Home Moon
or as Quiet Moon,
the right time, to mediate
and be grateful for the blessings of the past
and curious about the adventures of the year.

FIRST FULL MOON

a Lü Shi

First full moon in the new year,
a night so bright as day light,
big like a lantern in a lane,
jasmine rice steam rises from cook shops,
Wolves howl into the void, nocturnal sounds,
not disturbing the sleep of hibernating creatures,
moon stands high now on the firmament,
I continue my sleep, rest under blanket.

AUTUMN MOON

Blossom and leaf know change and turn,
earth days see constant beginning and end;
hold the spark of eternal fire in hand,
smile at vanishing years,
ignore the tick of the clock,
take the staff and continue to walk
the road, the steep winding stairs.

People are scattered like leaves by storm.
World fires blaze, and death reaps on earth.
Preserve this flame of mysterious birth,
which knows no decay, only lasting desire,
whose agony is lost in blissful devotion.
From a flowering exuberant explosion
incense clouds of sweetness emanate.

Time dissolves easily, so full of sun,
drink from the scarlet chalice of this day.
Gently, the linden tree hangs an array
over us: its subtle green filigree veils.
Chimes, in the distance, sound,
hours like fluttering leaves fall to the ground

slowly on the counting weighing scales.

Darkish and solemn under bitter air
leaves rustle on the narrow path,
announcing early autumn days.
Sweetly suffused by ripe apples' scent,
trees stretch their bronze-golden branches.
Wine winds purple chains around walls,
so rich and ripe, so full, this summer's end.

Shining like last bouquets
embraces summer selves in final love,
whispers goodbye; the cooing of a dove,
the heavy perfume of saved hay,
silage, straw, cabbage, and apples,
of pumpkins and grapes;
sustenance for long cold winter days.

LATE HARVEST MOON

Through a greenish curtain shot a spark.
Now it is gone. What's bothering my heart?
Colourful summer burned to the ground,
sun-kissed in golden deaths.
A withered mound of humus found
to pave the path for flora's birth.

How may we walk so lost in thoughts
through tawny meadows' band?
Over us, free, untamed across
wide clouds of light expand.

And all around the pale, discoloured world
in a contemplative farewell stillness,
as if in every leaf impressed
a holy fate is silently fulfilled.

Footsteps sound through silent hours,
breathless, anxious. Moon stands bright.
Above us, waving, longing, drunken,
aurora borealis sheds its northern light.

FALLOW MOON

Summer winds waft with heavy scents
through acacia's foliage crown,
with lilac, primrose fragrance blends,
a leaf comes loose and tumbles to the ground.

Summer flares off, like fire in a storm.
Wreaths wither, rot away, transform.
Midday blaze scorches now the garden,
armoured figures threaten, clandestine,
gigantic and grey, a wake for the sun
around the heaven's hem of silver shine.

A wrathful summer paces, thundering
night after night, through thirsty fields.
A dome above of lightning, blazing;
Below us, are illuminated, dark grey peaks.

Nights, when shooting stars begin to rain
sultry from the daytime pain,
wind-tossed treetops joining forces
like a herd of wild black horses.
Sweet-scented flowers on a darkish meadow,

dropping minutes vanish in their fragrance,
slow, like gentle honeydew.

HAY MOON's MORN and EVE

Mellow are the July nights,
when the sunset's reddish fading
and the early morning lights
dawning blur and blend.
When summer with red roses
bleeds to death so rapidly,
cawing ravens mourn the dead,
the blackbird has not sung
its last song yet.

Warm rays from the sunset
make distant peaks glow red,
the scream of the wild eagle
sounds over the forest silhouette,
while pale-cold falls the mist
into the closing day.

Under lime trees, under elms,
under thatched roof's hanging wings
overgrown with moss and weeds,
stretching wide and shielding.
I want to put it into a song

what on the moonlit village green
I heard the fairies lisping.
What grey stone's mossy green
inscription said to me.

Fog pictures rise in the twilight,
from the dark days 'past.
I hear faint voices whispering,
sounds of pleasure, lament, anger.
A last farewell, so distant.
Silent night in the deep forest
around the birches' black-white bark;
around the alder's trunks so dark,
flows the moonlight soft and mild.

CHANGING MOON

Summer, so soon,
wild strawberries grow
under your bright lamp
which is shining all night,
the full Strawberry Moon,
as signal and call
to harvest the ripening fruits.

July's full moon,
a month so full of light.
The summer flames up,
the wind wafts hot
through the crowns,
treetop replete with sunshine.
Singeing the barley fields
in the midday sun.

August blesses with raised hands.
Pollen rises like incense.
A solemn mood, full of awe.
Flowers' blossom will soon wither.
The willow hangs over the river.

The nights are sultry,
shooting stars fall, the air is still,
the asters sway in longing.

So sunmatt, rich and mature,
swells the ripe apples' smell.
In the cloud shadow, I rest,
so dreamdazed, sweet-inebriated.
Flaming on the hillside, the summer flees.
The reapers' song tune,
sustained by the sound of the sickle,
the steel crescent,
competing with the waxing moon.

SNOW MOON

Wind from the north-west
grooms the wild lyme grass.
We observe the sky,
contemplate the moon's shine,
enjoy the crickets' choir,
they sing into the night.
To prevent a fall
your hand rests in mine.

STRAWBERRY MOON

I look up from my book of poetry
and see your 'seek and hide' play.
You peek through the *Reeks*' valley
then rise like a released balloon,
let loose over the mountain range
on this night in June
and pour a pink glow
over the slopes and a lonely grange.

You are so close to us now
on your elliptical path.
So peaceful, so feminine, 'Luna'.
Not like your wild brother 'Sol'.
So round and full,
filling the sleeper's dreams.
Moving the ocean waves,
silently rocking the world
casting gentle shadows.

LONE MOON

The sun tells a lie in the morning,
gainsays us the fading night, the dawn,
when it is rising soft and rosy
still in her sleeping gown,
chasing away the old grumpy moon,
who kept watch the whole boring night,
fearing he would be laughed at
because he looks into many windows
and feels neither pleasure nor fun.

Compared with a human being
as people speak of the man in the moon,
when, on the night sky,
they see him sailing, this quiet balloon,
marking the ingress or egress
of the night and the day,
he is so triste and pale,
so colourless and bloodless,
so nightlone.

A MOONLIGHT NIGHT

Strange, the darkness,
strange, the forest,
strange the rock at *Ard-na-Sidhe,*
on which the fascinating moon casts silver coins
to wake up a flustered fairy,
who gathers moments in a wicker basket
to feed dream fish
in *Caragh Lake.*

IRISH FULL MOON

I see you in the dark firmament
like a sallow lantern,
over the *MacGillycuddy's Reeks,*
your bright round face
gives me joy and peace.
You do not make me blink
or dazzle me,
a planet mild and pale
in a sea of black ink,
makes its way across the sky,
strides along, silent and shy.

I would like to paint you green
to match the landscape,
copy for you the sheen
of these fresh slopes, the fields,
all the emerald shades
that here exist,
then release you over the peaks
or let you sink behind them,
so that after your journey
you rise again

above the mountains
and cast a silver shine
upon them.

MOON over MONGOLIA

Blue sky pulls white cloud curtains
night closes brushwood door.
I bear pain and loneliness,
look at the moon, golden hoar.
Behind the door, tea is bubbling.
Felt doors open gently, invite.
Dream blown away by the wind,
frost from early winter night.

WAXING GIBBOUS

The moon's crescent can be seen,
then obscured by wintery clouds,
as behind a screen,
later accompanied by stars
on an ice-cold, starry sky.
Much has happened: bad news,
distress, uncertainty, tears.

Hoarfrost lies on hearts,
Far away and yet close,
feelings, compassionate,
are shared
then a silver lining appeared.
Waves, vibes, a lot of sent energy
take effect, are there.

PINK MOON

I can read in the night,
the pink moon shines so bright
From book pages lift effortlessly
letters that learn to speak and walk
on such a nocturnal sky.

They tell me about angels' metal wings,
and their unique nature
and their billions of years
in the universe -
sometimes here, sometimes there,
to see, to locate, to sow, to harvest,
travelling in incomprehensible infinity,
bringing salvation,
prune, legislate, create.

Moon, with your ancient glow.
As old as the universe,
as old as knowledge,
as renewable,
your all-monthly glow.

THE DAY PASSES

The day passes.
Evening birds sit on the branches.
We live amid mountains and lakes,
forests, a wonder, a paradise.
Our dreams swing up, winged,
to the moon that hangs
over the mountain range
like a round Chinese lantern.
The light of stars, long past, arrives
sparkling and speaks to us
of endless times
and millions of years of travel,
makes our escape from Earth impossible,
shatters the dream,
however
reminds us to preserve,
love it, cherish and maintain.
We are alone in space
because *K2-18b*, this habitable planet,
is 124 light years away from us
and we have nothing else in our hands
but coming and going sunny days

and vanishing moonlight on summer nights.
Let us hold on
as long as the sun shines,
from which we only borrow light,
life and warmth,
until we become burnt,
then frozen star clusters.
Once upon a time.
In a few million years!

MAY MOON 1st of May

A sickle on a cloudless sky
and, underneath, bright
like a punctuation mark
the Venus – a light
near the gentle face of the moon
soon,
at midnight into the spring we glide,
long for the blossoming trees.
Bonfires are lit in the night:
purification, healing, renewal, spiritual light.
The beginning of summer.
Beltene, the "fires of Bel", "bright fire",
we venerate Belenus, the solar deity,
wear garlands of flowers, rowan branches,
to ward off malevolent spirits
this liminal time,
when the boundary between us
and the otherworld is thin
we celebrate the thriving nature
under the flower moon,
the abundant ornature.

Celtic mystical Beltane poem:

THE FIRE of BEL

Under the rising Flower Moon
on *Uisneach*'s hill the flames are lit,
where dusk and dawn dancing meet,
between the fires the cattle are led,
to purify, give health and strength.

The veil is thin between the worlds,
the spirits rise from silent sleep.
We weave the wreath with rowan red,
to ward off the evil's threat

Hawthorn's white cluster,
thorny with lobed leaves,
foxglove, a violet mark,
gorse abloom, in yellow splendour
marks the entrance to **fairy realms**.

The Queen of May, in a floral dress,
a fleeting beauty of spring and youth
meets Green Man in leafy attire.
Woods and fields with song resound
sacred union, **life and death intertwined**,
reminder of our place in the natural order.

Light the fire, let passion rise,
on earth below and starry skies.
For Beltane's breath is vital and bright—
A kiss of flame, the flower moon at night.

MAY BLOSSOM MOON

O May moon, gentle lantern high,
as white pink plate in the dark sky,
you crown the month with petal lights,
in almond blossom scented nights,
where branches pale with ghostly lace
stretch out to feel your shining grace.

All earth is song beneath your glow—
Each bud, each leaf begins to grow,
the lilac, roses, rhododendrons show.
Cherry trees with bridal arms
embrace the dusk with scented charms;
their blossoms tumble in the breeze,
as white prayers on the moonlit fields.

A thousand flowers raise their heads
and bloom beneath your watching face.
Flower Moon, May's month's delight,
sheds silver, gentle shine so bright—
You bloom in us what dares to be,
hope, new beginning, harmony.

SAKURA FLOWER MOON

Under the glow of the Flower Moon,
white pink cherry tree petals bloom—
A feast of spring and fragrant sky,
where spirits dance and fly.
The night wears silk of silver hue,
when the moon spills silver light,
casts shadows, tender and true.
As cherry blossoms gently snow,
like fleeting dreams, the full moon swells
Beneath this glow, the earth rests,
and time forgets its hurried pace,
And in the sky, the night adorned,
a promise made, a vow re-sworn,
under the Flower Moon's glow,
we are reborn.

I think a poem is never finished, I always see it as a sculpture, or, better, as a rough ashlar that a poet, like a stonemason, is working on, polishing here, removing something there, creating a new contour, knocking off excrescences (or imperfections), rough edges, turning the rough ashlar into a smooth and perfect stone to fit into a structure.
That is how poems go through different phases for me; I see them and work on them under different lights.

Here is a poem in a philosophical form:

WOLF MOON MEDITATION

The forest, steeped in nocturnal grey,
draped in veils of moss and lichens,
like shrouds waiting for spring,
passing relics of winter's repose.
The secret communication of roots,
from tree to tree,
first mushrooms grow in clearings
as a fairy ring.
The world abides in a somnolent dusk:
grey sky, grey soil, grey bark, grey husk.

Night descends,
the ancient game unfolds:
Mars, red messenger of battles and wars,
red, at the right of the Wolf Moon,
a sentinel of the sleeping world,
night's keyholder for *Luna*,
the sun, that source of heat,
rises in the East and sets in the West —
an eternal rhythm, for millions of years,
one star of a multitude in the vast universe.

Likewise, the Moon, the lesser light,
rises in the East to monitor our dreams,
to cradle our fugitive selves in its care,
before wandering westwards,
reminding us
that all things are constantly in motion,
following an eternal law.

The mountain range —
a line drawn with a piece of chalk
across a darkish canvas —
under the Moon's argent lustre,
where the green-white fields
are strewn with silver dust.

And at the Moon's side stands Mars,
a drop of blood on the pale robe of night.
The earth sleeps the sleep of the just
as do deer, fox, badgers, hedgehogs
in forests and distant valleys.

I stand,
and breathe the piercing air,
of the silent wilderness.
The world is bathed
in a sea of silver light.

We who observe all from below,
feel the pull of cosmic dance
within the marrow of our bones.
And when the celestial waltz concludes,
we, too, retreat —
not in sorrow, but in profound gratitude:
naming the Moon with reverence —
Stay Home Moon, Quiet Moon —
for it teaches us to pause,
to ponder what has been bestowed.
Beneath this dome of the firmament,
the soul, too, is called to contemplate,
to be still, to be hopeful, to retreat.

Or a mystical-philosophical version:

WOLF MOON HYMN

The rising morning
prepares for the day.
The horizon is still grey –
sandstone slopes, heather, forests, –
all dressed in the same colours.

Their greyish demureness
reassures deer, badger and deer
stoat, hare and marten
they hark into the silence.

Spring hesitates, winter still prevails:
frost clings to the forest edges,
roots dream in frozen soil,
trees communicate, send messages
through the underground mycelium.
In the dusk, a red star still stands.

Mars, companion, sword bearer,
sides the Wolf Moon,
Both vigil to greet the sun
to hand over the day key
to open the door for the sun.

All ascend to descend,
and descend to ascend anew.
The mountain chain,
a white line against heaven,
catches the Moon's silver hem.
Fields still bear the hoarfrost
the mountains wear a snow cloak,
deer startle, foxes cry,
wolves call out their loneliness.
Above, the Moon and Mars,
two voyagers in the dawn.

Tonight, the heaven turns
with patient hands
the pages of an old book,
that offers no answers but prophecies.
And we, beneath the cold Moon,
gather in gratitude —
for the countless times of light,
and for the mysteries ahead,
for the time of being
in a world where nothing stays
and everything constantly changes.

An esoteric and symbolic version:

FROM the BOOK of the WOLF MOON

The Earth veiled in nocturnal shrouds
in some parts of the earth,
where people sleep into the next day.

Dark blue hangs the sky.
The landscape forgot its colour,
for a short time
until the Sun rises again
and the Moon descends
behind the curvature of the horizon.
The two mystic round plates
one golden, the other one silver,
are on their way.
Mars approaches in a red robe,
this ancient warrior.
The mountains lie still,
the fields wear silver silk,
the birds sleep, the deer hide.
No wolf howls.
The soul reposes.

Above,
the Moon, Mars, Venus,
lightyears away,
send a message to us

to show us how small we are
in this endless universe.
Tonight, the Wolf Moon reigns.

MOON HAIKU and TANKA

early sunset
puts blanket over green fields
full moon silvering the *Reeks*
last summer day makes heart heavy
we bewail lost time and warmth

early winter night frost--
the door opening gently
a framed **pale moon**

look at the **kind moon**,
round like a crisp healthy bread
promising deep sleep

lights extinguish
windows darken, close their eyes
moon wakes up

door opens gently
an early winter night frost
pale moon in doorframe

chinese pastry moon cake
dark sky copies sweet delights
makes me sleepy

lunar poems
I pull **a moon**
from the night

remains of a dream
moonlight a pale mountain hem
steam of a morning tea

dawn silence
paints golden stripes
on dark **moon sky**

bright polished **full moon**
pouring gold light over fields
bark of a lone dog

hissing and panting
these celestial horses
dawn at a full moon

early winter night frost--
the door, opening gently
a framed **pale moon**

new moon
a blue horse
in a field

Here are **different names and terms for the Moon**, originating from various cultures, languages, and poetic references:

1. **Luna** – Latin origin, commonly used in English and other languages.
2. **Selene** – Greek goddess of the Moon.
3. **Chandra** – Sanskrit name for the Moon in Hinduism.
4. **Artemis** – Greek goddess associated with the Moon, especially about the hunt.
5. **Cynthia** – Another name for Artemis, reflecting her association with the Moon.
6. **Tsukiyo** – Japanese word for "moonlit night."
7. **Mana** – Polynesian name for the Moon, sometimes considered a deity.
8. **Hecate** – Greek goddess of the Moon, magic, and witchcraft.
9. **Khonsu** – Egyptian god of the Moon.
10. **Qamar** – Arabic name for the Moon.
11. **Shashi** – Hindi name for the Moon.
12. **Máni** – Norse mythology, personifying the Moon.
13. **Mēnē** – Latin word for the Moon, used in ancient texts.
14. **Sin** – Ancient Mesopotamian god of the Moon.

15. **Moonbeam** – A poetic term for the light reflected from the Moon.
16. **Silver Lady** – A poetic and romantic reference to the Moon.
17. **Lunaria** – Derived from the term "Luna," often used in poetic contexts.

Here are the different names for the full moons throughout the year, often linked to seasonal events, activities, and nature:

1. **Wolf Moon** – January: January's full wolf moon is named after the howling of wolves in midwinter. Other names are: old moon and ice moon.
2. **Snow Moon** – February: Named after heavy snowfall that occurs during February. Storm moon and hunger moon are other names.
3. **Worm Moon** – March: Native Americans called this last full winter moon the worm moon after worm trails in the thawed ground. Other names are chaste moon, death moon, crust moon and sap moon, after tapping the maple trees.
4. **Pink Moon** – April: Named after the pink flowers, among them f.e. the wild phlox, that bloom in spring.
5. **Flower Moon** – May: After the abundance of the month's flowers or as reference to May's full moon as the flower moon thanks to the abundant spring blooming. Other names are: the hare moon, the corn planting moon, or the milk moon.

6. **Strawberry Moon** – June: The strawberry harvest season. This moon was called the rose moon, or the hot moon for the beginning of the summer heat.
7. **Buck Moon** – July: Refers to the time when male deer (bucks) begin growing their antlers. Male deer, (bucks) begin to regrow their antlers in July. Some call this moon thunder moon, because of the summer storms in July.
8. **Sturgeon Moon** – August: Named for the large sturgeon fish. Fishing tribes called August's full moon the sturgeon moon since the species appeared in number during this month. It's also been called the green corn moon, the grain moon, and the red moon for the reddish hue it often takes on in the summer haze.
9. **Corn Moon** – September: September's full corn moon during the time of the crops gathering at the end of the summer season. Around September the moon appears bright and rises early and gives farmers the possibility to harvest in the night. This moon is also called the barley moon and is the nearest full moon to the autumnal equinox, therefore the title of 'harvest moon'.
10. **Harvest Moon** – September/October: The harvest moon refers to the nearest full moon to the autumnal

equinox. The light of the Harvest Moon allows farmers to harvest late into the night. Mostly in September.

11. **Hunter's Moon** – October, when hunters would hunt to stock up food for the winter. The hunter's moon follows the Harvest Moon. The hunter's moon stands bright and long in the sky, giving hunters the opportunity to hunt at night.
12. **Beaver Moon** – November: There is disagreement over the origin of November's beaver moon name. Some say it comes from Native Americans setting beaver traps during this month, while others say the name comes from the heavy activity of beavers building their winter dams. Another name is the frost moon.
13. **Cold Moon** – December: The December's full moon is called the cold moon.

How many phases of the Moon are there?

These are the banana-shaped crescent Moon, the D-shaped quarter Moon and the almost complete gibbous Moon.

Each phase is also named after its position in the full 29.5-day cycle based on whether it is growing (waxing) or shrinking (waning).

The eight phases of the moon are:

1. new moon
2. waxing crescent moon
3. first quarter moon
4. waxing gibbous moon
5. full moon
6. waning gibbous moon
7. last quarter moon
8. waning crescent moon.

About the Author

Eduard Schmidt-Zorner is certainly an accomplished and multitalented writer and translator! His proficiency in four languages allows him to engage with a diverse range of literary traditions and audiences.

It's impressive how extensively his work has been published across the globe, reflecting a widespread appreciation for his poetry and prose.

His dedication to traditional forms like haiku and haibun, but also to poetry, short stories, literary thrillers, and experimental poetry showcases his versatility and creative range.

Living in County Kerry/Ireland for over three decades, he is deeply rooted in the Irish literary community, contributing significantly to its richness and diversity.

His penname, **Eadbhard McGowan**, adds another layer of intrigue to his identity as a writer.

Overall, his contributions to literature and poetry are extensive and diverse, reflecting a rich tapestry of linguistic and cultural influences.

Moon over the MacGillycuddy's Reeks. A view from my window

www.ingramcontent.com/pod-product-compliance
Ingram Content Group UK Ltd.
Pitfield, Milton Keynes, MK11 3LW, UK
UKHW041316190726
13845UKWH00025B/314